# THE BIG BOOK
# OF WILD CATS

# THE BIG BOOK OF WILD CATS

## Fun Animal Facts for Kids

Rachael Smith

**Illustrations by Boris Stoilov**

ROCKRIDGE
PRESS

For general information on our other products and services or to obtain technical support, please contact our Customer Care Department within the United States at (866) 744-2665, or outside the United States at (510) 253-0500.

Rockridge Press publishes its books in a variety of electronic and print formats. Some content that appears in print may not be available in electronic books, and vice versa.

Interior and Cover Designer: Linda Snorina
Art Producer: Michael Hardgrove
Editor: Andrea Leptinsky
Production Editor: Emily Sheehan

Illustrations: Boris Stoilov

Interior art used under license from © Shutterstock.com & iStockphoto.com.

Author photo courtesy of © Jamie Healy.

ISBN: Print 978-1-64611-060-5
eBook 978-1-64611-061-2

R0

To my husband, Kyle, and
our four wonderful kids:
Thanks for making life
a wildly fun adventure!

# Contents

# THE SMALL CATS 31

# Introduction

In this book you will learn fascinating facts about 37 different **species** of wild cats! They can be found all over the world, with cats living on every continent except Antarctica. Wild cats can be as large as 600 pounds, like a tiger, or as tiny as just a few pounds, like the black-footed cat. No matter the size of the cat, they are **carnivores** and fierce hunters. Depending on the size of the cat and where they live, they eat many different types of animals. Some hunt tiny mice and birds while others hunt deer or antelope. Some cats can swim underwater to snag their **prey**, and others can leap high into the air to snatch a bird in flight.

Wild cats can be found in all types of **habitats**, from snowy mountains to scorching-hot deserts. They have different **adaptations** to help them survive in their specific environment. From huge paws that work like snowshoes to rotating ankles that help them climb down trees, their bodies are built to survive the conditions they face.

Cats are an important part of our world's ecosystem; they keep populations of prey animals, such as rodents, under control. Can you imagine if there were mice everywhere? Cats help keep these pests under control so that they don't take over our crops or spread diseases.

You may be used to seeing house cats, but in this book, you will discover many secretive wild cats that you may have never heard of. They come in a variety of sizes, and many have stunning coat patterns. One fact applies to these 37 wild cats: Their different skills will amaze you!

# CATS AROUND THE WORLD

## FROM BIGGEST TO SMALLEST

**Tiger:** Tigers can grow up to 10 feet long and weigh between 220 and 660 pounds.

**Lion:** Lions can grow 4.5 to 6.5 feet long and weigh between 265 and 420 pounds.

**Jaguar:** Jaguars can grow 5 to 6 feet long and weigh between 100 and 250 pounds.

**Leopard:** Leopards can grow up to about 6 feet long and weigh up to 176 pounds.

**Cougar:** Cougars can grow 3.25 to 5.25 feet long and weigh up to 250 pounds.

**Snow Leopard:** Snow leopards can grow from 4 to 5 feet long and weigh between 60 and 120 pounds.

**Cheetah:** Cheetahs can grow 3.5 to 4.5 feet long and weigh up to 140 pounds.

**Sunda Clouded Leopard:** Sunda clouded leopards can grow 27 to 41 inches long and weigh between 22 and 55 pounds.

TIGER

JAGUAR

IBERIAN LYNX

RUSTY-SPOTTED CAT

**Clouded Leopard:** Clouded leopards can grow 27 to 42 inches long and weigh between 24 and 50 pounds.

**Eurasian Lynx:** The Eurasian lynx can grow 31 to 43 inches long and weigh between 33 and 64 pounds.

**Caracal:** Caracals can grow 24 to 42 inches long and weigh between 13 and 44 pounds.

**Canada Lynx:** The Canada lynx can grow 30 to 42 inches long and weigh between 11 and 37 pounds.

**Asian Golden Cat:** Asian golden cats can grow 26 to 41 inches long and weigh up to 33 pounds.

**Fishing Cat:** Fishing cats can grow 22 to 45 inches long and weigh between 11 and 31 pounds.

**Bobcat:** Bobcats can grow 26 to 41 inches long and weigh between 11 and 30 pounds.

**African Golden Cat:** African golden cats can grow 24 to 37 inches long and weigh between 24 and 30 pounds.

**Serval:** Servals can grow 23 to 36 inches long and weigh between 15 and 40 pounds.

**Ocelot:** Ocelots can grow 28 to 35 inches long and weigh between 24 and 35 pounds.

**Wildcat:** Wildcats can grow 16 to 36 inches long and weigh between 6 and 18 pounds.

**Chinese Mountain Cat:** Chinese mountain cats can grow 27 to 33 inches long and weigh between 10 and 20 pounds.

**Iberian Lynx:** The Iberian lynx can grow 27 to 32 inches long and weigh between 15 and 22 pounds.

**Jungle Cat:** Jungle cats can grow 23 to 30 inches long and weigh between 11 and 20 pounds.

**Geoffroy's Cat:** Geoffroy's cats can grow 17 to 34 inches long and weigh between 6 and 13 pounds.

**Jaguarundi:** Jaguarundis can grow 21 to 30 inches long and weigh between 6 and 15 pounds.

**Pampas Cat:** Pampas cats can grow 16.5 to 31 inches long and weigh between 6.6 and 9 pounds.

**Leopard Cat:** Leopard cats can grow 18 to 29 inches long and weigh between 4 and 15 pounds.

**Borneo Bay Cat:** Borneo bay cats can grow 21 to 27 inches long and weigh between 6 and 9 pounds.

**Margay:** Margays can grow 18 to 27 inches long and weigh between 5 and 11 pounds.

**Pallas's Cat:** Pallas's cats can grow 18 to 26 inches long and weigh between 5 and 13 pounds.

**Andean Mountain Cat:** Andean mountain cats can grow 22 to 25 inches long and weigh between 8 and 13 pounds.

**Marbled Cat:** Marbled cats can grow 18 to 24 inches long and weigh between 4.4 and 11 pounds.

**Oncilla:** Oncillas can grow 15 to 23 inches long and weigh between 3.3 and 6.6 pounds.

**Sand Cat:** Sand cats can grow 15 to 20 inches long and weigh between 3 and 7.5 pounds.

**Kodkod:** Kodkods can grow 14 to 20 inches long and weigh between 3.3 and 6.6 pounds.

**Flat-headed Cat:** Flat-headed cats can grow 13 to 20 inches long and weigh between 3 and 6 pounds.

**Black-footed Cat:** Black-footed cats can grow 14 to 20 inches long and weigh between 2.4 to 4.2 pounds.

**Rusty-spotted Cat:** Rusty-spotted cats can grow 13 to 19 inches long and weigh between 2 and 3.5 pounds.

# WHO WINS THE RACE?

**Can you guess which cat is the world's fastest?**

It's the cheetah!

Cheetahs can reach speeds of up to 70 miles per hour in just 3 seconds. They are the fastest land animals on earth!

# Honorable Mentions

Want to know the runners-up? These cats cannot outrun a cheetah, but they are still extremely fast!

**Lions** can run at speeds up to 50 miles per hour! These massive cats can get their huge bodies moving quickly with powerful strides.

**Servals** can also run at speeds up to 50 miles per hour. Not only are these cats quick, but they can leap more than 9 feet into the air to snatch a bird!

**Jaguars** can get to a top speed of 50 miles per hour. Combine their incredible speed with the strongest bite of any cat, and it's easy to see why these cats are fierce hunters!

**Caracals** can accelerate to speeds up to 50 miles per hour. They can also use their strong legs to jump over 10 feet high. They could easily jump over a grown adult!

**Cougars** can run up to 50 miles per hour. They can also leap forward 15 feet in a single bound. This lets them quickly cross the rocky terrain of their habitat.

**Tigers** can grow to over 600 pounds, but these cats can still reach speeds up to 40 miles per hour. They can also leap forward up to 30 feet in a single bound!

These wild cats can outrun a human. The fastest human has a recorded speed of nearly 28 miles per hour! On average, healthy adult humans can run around 10 to 15 miles per hour.

Cougar

# THE BIG CATS

The big cats are large, fierce hunters built to take down large prey. These cats range in size from around 50 pounds to over 600 pounds. They all have excellent hunting techniques as well as sharp claws and teeth. While most of the big cats can roar, some cannot. Many of these gigantic cats are on the **endangered** species list, as there are only small numbers of them alive, and their populations may continue to decrease.

Ready to meet the big cats?

First up is the speedy cheetah, who can reach speeds of up to 70 miles an hour! Then you will read all about the long-tailed clouded leopard, as well as the mighty leopard, secretive snow leopard, and the Sunda clouded leopard. You'll learn about cougars and their amazing ability to jump. Then the jaguar, whose jaws are strong enough to pierce a turtle's shell! Next you will meet the ferocious lion, whose loud roar can be heard for miles. Last, but not least, is the beautiful tiger, whose massive size doesn't stop it from being a speedy and agile hunter.

# Cheetah

*Acinonyx jubatus*

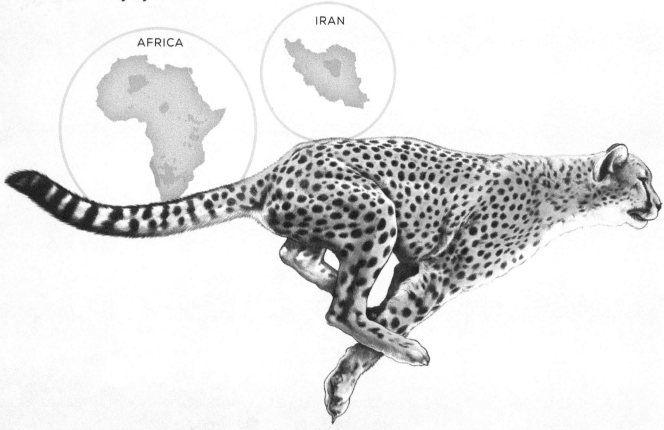

AFRICA

IRAN

## FAST FACTS

**SIZE:** 3.5 to 4.5 feet long; up to 140 pounds

**LIFE SPAN:** 10 to 12 years

**FOOD:** Rabbits, birds, antelope, and the young of larger animals

**SOUNDS:** Purrs, barks, growls, hisses, and chirps

## APPEARANCE

Cheetahs have tan or yellow fur with dark spots covering most of their bodies. They have white fur on their bellies. Cheetahs have slender bodies built for speed.

## HABITAT

Cheetahs live throughout Africa. They can be found roaming open **savanna** plains and open forests. A tiny population of Asiatic cheetahs remains in Iran.

## RAISING YOUNG

Female cheetahs give birth to an average of three to six cubs each litter. The cubs average 9 to 12 ounces at birth and stay with their mother until about 18 months old. During the time they spend with their mother, the cubs learn to hunt.

## SOCIAL STRUCTURE

Unlike other large cats, adult female cheetahs tend to be **solitary**, while the adult males live in small groups called "coalitions." These coalitions are usually formed from male littermates that stay together as they reach adulthood. The female littermates go off on their own at around 2 years of age. Females remain alone until they find mates and have their own litters of cubs.

## HUNTING HABITS

Cheetahs are **diurnal**, which means they primarily hunt during the day. This helps them avoid competition from lions, hyenas, and leopards. Cheetahs also have excellent eyesight so they can spot prey from far distances. Since their bursts of speed use so much energy, they usually creep to within 100 yards of prey before beginning the chase. Cheetahs are successful in half of their hunting attempts.

Even though they are successful hunters, cheetahs sometimes get bullied out of their meals by other carnivores. In order to ensure they don't lose their meals, cheetahs tend to eat quickly. Cheetahs hunt for rabbits, birds, antelope, and the young of larger animals.

## COMMUNICATION

Cheetahs can't roar like other big cats. One of the most common sounds cheetahs use is chirping. Their chirps can be heard from a mile away! The sound of their chirp has been compared to the chirp of a bird or a dog's yelp. They use this sound to communicate a variety of things, such as trying to reunite with their group, indicating they are distressed, or trying to attract a mate. Other sounds that cheetahs make are purrs, stutters, barks, growls, and hisses.

## SPEED

Cheetahs are the fastest land animal. They can reach speeds of 60 to 70 miles per hour! They accelerate fast, making them successful in catching their speedy prey. Cheetahs can only maintain a high speed for about 300 yards, so their hunts end quickly.

# Clouded Leopard

*Neofelis nebulosa*

SOUTHEAST ASIA

## FAST FACTS

**SIZE:** 27 to 42 inches long; 24 to 50 pounds

**LIFE SPAN:** 12 to 15 years

**FOOD:** Deer, wild pigs, monkeys, rodents, and birds

**SOUNDS:** Growls, hisses, and chuffs

## APPEARANCE

Clouded leopards get their names from their beautiful cloud-shaped spots. They are light brown with patterns of dark stripes and blotches all over their bodies. Clouded leopards are rarely seen in the wild, due to their superb ability to climb and excellent camouflage. They have a very long tail, which helps them keep their balance. Adult male clouded leopards are much larger than females. Males weigh up to 50 pounds, while females usually weigh just 25 to 35 pounds.

## RAISING YOUNG

Female clouded leopards can give birth to one to five cubs in a litter, but they usually have two or three. Cubs are helpless at birth and rely on their mother for milk. They open their eyes about 2 weeks after they are born. As they grow, their mother teaches them to hunt. They usually leave their mother to go off on their own at around 2 years old.

## PARTICULAR SKILLS

Clouded leopards have large paws built for climbing. They also have special ankle bones that allow them to easily climb down a tree headfirst. Their amazing paws also allow them to hang upside down from tree branches. These features make them one of the best climbers in the cat family. Clouded leopards are also good swimmers.

## HUNTING HABITS

When sharing hunting grounds with larger **predators** such as tigers or jaguars, clouded leopards hunt at night to avoid competition. But in areas that the larger predators aren't around, clouded leopards hunt during the day. Clouded leopards have very long canine teeth relative to their size. Their canines are 2 inches long—the same size as a tiger's fangs! They can also open their mouths extremely wide. Their fierce teeth and wide jaw help them kill prey. Clouded Leopards do most of their hunting on the ground, but may also hunt in trees. Clouded leopards eat deer, wild pigs, monkeys, rodents, and birds.

## HABITAT

Clouded leopards live in Southeast Asia. They are mostly found living in tropical **rain forests** but some have been found in **grasslands**, **scrublands**, and wetland habitats. Their rain forest habitats are getting smaller since humans are taking more of their land for farming and logging.

## POPULATION

Since clouded leopards are secretive cats, scientists are unsure of the exact number living in the wild. They are considered vulnerable on the endangered species list. It is illegal to hunt clouded leopards, but some people still hunt them for their fur.

# Cougar

*Puma concolor*

NORTH
AMERICA

SOUTH
AMERICA

## FAST FACTS

**SIZE:** 3.25 to 5.25 feet long; up
to 250 pounds

**LIFE SPAN:** Up to 20 years

**FOOD:** Deer, coyotes, raccoons,
and porcupines

**SOUNDS:** Growls, hisses,
meows, yowls, squeaks,
whistles, purrs, and even short,
high-pitched screams

## APPEARANCE

Cougars are usually a solid tawny color with slightly darker fur on their backs and white fur on their bellies. Their colors vary slightly based on the environment that they live in. Cougars have strong back legs used for jumping. They also have large paws and supersharp claws!

## RAISING YOUNG

Like many other large cats, cougars are mostly solitary creatures besides when they mate or while raising their cubs. Female cougars usually find a cave or shelter of some sort to give birth. She can have anywhere between one and six cubs at a time, but the average is two to three. When cougar cubs are born, they have spots that eventually fade. By 6 weeks of age, they can start eating some of the meat their mother brings back from a hunt. Cubs stay with their mothers for a year or two as they learn how to hunt.

## HABITAT

Cougars can be found from North America to South America. In fact, their range is larger than any other land animal in the Western Hemisphere! Since cougars live in so many places, they have gotten many different names from various cultures. They are also known as panthers, pumas, mountain lions, and catamounts. Cougars require a lot of space, and only a few cougars can inhabit a large area. Sometimes their ranges overlap, but only a few cougars can live within a 30-mile radius.

## PARTICULAR SKILLS

Cougars have great eyesight and use this to spot their prey from a distance. They also have great jumping skills and can even leap from the ground up into a tree!

## HUNTING HABITS

Cougars mostly hunt deer, but also eat smaller animals like coyotes, raccoons, and porcupines. They are ambush hunters, sneaking up close to their prey and stalking them prior to attack. Once they get close enough, cougars launch at their prey and knock it off balance, then use their strong jaws to bite the animal's neck. If they have leftover meat from a kill, cougars will hide or bury it so that they can feast on it at a later time. Cougars are **crepuscular**, which means that they are most active at dawn and dusk.

## POPULATION

Cougars used to live throughout most of the United States, but hunting has nearly eliminated them from the East and Midwest. A very small population of Florida panthers still live in Florida, but they are considered endangered.

The rest of the cougar population is not on the threatened species list, and they can be found from British Columbia in Canada all the way through the continent of South America.

# Jaguar

*Panthera onca*

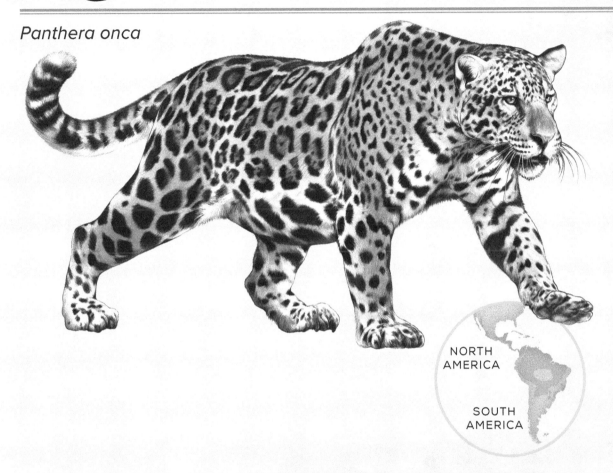

NORTH
AMERICA

SOUTH
AMERICA

## FAST FACTS

**SIZE:** 5 to 6 feet long; 100 to
250 pounds

**LIFE SPAN:** 12 to 15 years

**FOOD:** Deer, peccaries,
capybaras, turtles, and tapirs

**SOUNDS:** Roars, growls,
and meows

## APPEARANCE

Most jaguars have orange or tawny fur with black spots shaped like a rose, called rosettes. Some jaguars appear to be all black because they have dark fur all over their body. Even though these dark jaguars don't seem to have spots, their spots can usually be seen if you take a close look. Each jaguar has its own unique spot pattern. Jaguars and leopards look very similar in appearance and often people confuse the two. Jaguars are stockier and more muscular than leopards. Although both cats have rosettes, another difference between the two is that jaguars' rosettes have a spot in the center. Leopards do not have a spot in the center of their rosettes.

## RAISING YOUNG

Jaguars are solitary cats except when a female is raising her young. Female jaguars usually have between one and four cubs in a litter. The cubs are blind and completely dependent on their mothers at birth. Jaguar cubs learn from their mother during their first two years of life.

## HABITAT

Most jaguars live in remote areas of South and Central America. Jaguars have many skills that help them survive in their tropical rain forest habitat. They are excellent swimmers and climbers. They can also survive in grasslands and desert habitats.

## PARTICULAR SKILLS

Jaguars are often found by water as they hunt for aquatic animals. Some jaguars actually fish by gently waving and tapping their tail on the surface of the water to lure fish. Once the fish get close enough, the jaguar snatches them out of the water. Jaguars have excellent night vision and can see six times better than humans in the dark.

## HUNTING HABITS

Jaguars have extremely strong jaws! They attack by chomping down and piercing their prey's skull. Their jaws are strong enough to bite through a turtle shell and the thick hides of caimans. The name "jaguar" comes from the Native American word *yaguar*, which means "he who kills with one leap." Jaguars also hunt for land animals by climbing trees to pounce on their prey. They eat many different animals including deer, peccaries, capybaras, and tapirs.

## POPULATION

Only about 10,000 jaguars remain in the wild. With their natural habitat shrinking, the jaguar population is declining. Their habitat is shrinking because mining, logging, and farming are using the land jaguars use to roam. It is against the law to sell jaguar skin, but some people illegally hunt them for their attractive fur.

# Leopard

*Panthera pardus*

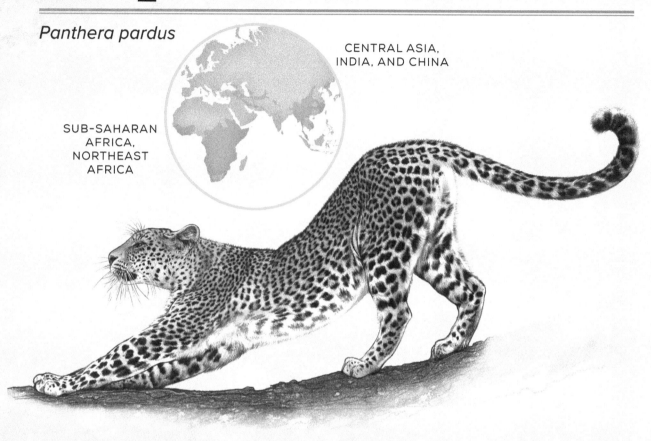

CENTRAL ASIA, INDIA, AND CHINA

SUB-SAHARAN AFRICA, NORTHEAST AFRICA

## FAST FACTS

**SIZE:** 4.25 to 6.25 feet long; up to 176 pounds

**LIFE SPAN:** 12 to 17 years

**FOOD:** A large variety of animals including fish and crabs

**SOUNDS:** Raspy coughs, purrs, and growls

## APPEARANCE

Leopards usually have light coats with dark rosettes. Their spots are called rosettes because the pattern has the shape of a rose. Leopards don't have a spot in the middle of their rosettes like jaguars do. Some leopards appear to be all black because they have dark fur with dark spots. Their spots help them blend into their surroundings so that they can creep up on prey.

## BEHAVIOR

Leopards are solitary cats, which means they spend most of their lives living alone. They are only seen together to mate, or while female leopards raise their young. Since they prefer to be alone, leopards mark their territory to tell other cats to stay away. Leopards are mainly **nocturnal** and do most of their hunting at night.

## RAISING YOUNG

Female leopards have two to three cubs at a time and keep them hidden in a cave, den, or thick **vegetation**. The cubs are born a grayish color, and their spots aren't very noticeable. Females raise the cubs on their own until the cubs are around 2 years old. Then they are capable of hunting and taking care of themselves.

## PARTICULAR SKILLS

Leopards are excellent climbers. They go up in trees to relax, hunt, or hide their food from scavengers. During the heat of the day they sprawl out and relax in tree branches. They have powerful legs that are perfect for making large leaps. They can jump forward about 20 feet! They use this skill to pounce on their unsuspecting prey. Leopards are also good swimmers who occasionally eat fish and crabs.

Leopards have a great sense of hearing. They can hear more pitches than humans can and pick up on sounds from much farther away.

## HABITAT

Leopards can adapt to live in many different habitats. They can live in nearly any kind of habitat and have been found roaming in rain forests, savannas, forests, and mountain habitats.

## HUNTING HABITS

Leopards have a lot of skills that make them excellent hunters. Leopards rarely do long chases to catch their prey. Instead, leopards sneak up on their prey until they get close enough to pounce. They do this by creeping through tree branches or crouching low beneath the grass and brush. Then they attack with a big leap and a strong bite. Leopards are very quick, with bursts of speed that can reach about 36 miles per hour! Once leopards get close to their prey, they attack fast! After a successful hunt, leopards are strong enough to drag their meal into a tree to keep it hidden from scavengers such as hyenas. Leopards are not picky eaters and will eat a wide variety of animals.

## POPULATION

Leopards are listed as vulnerable on the International Union for Conservation of Nature (IUCN) Red List of Threatened Species. This list keeps track of how severe the risk of extinction is, which is when there are no animals left on Earth in a species. All the subspecies of leopards are either endangered or threatened. The population of leopards is getting smaller because of habitat loss, illegal poaching, and ranchers poisoning the cats to keep them away from their livestock.

# Lion

*Panthera leo*

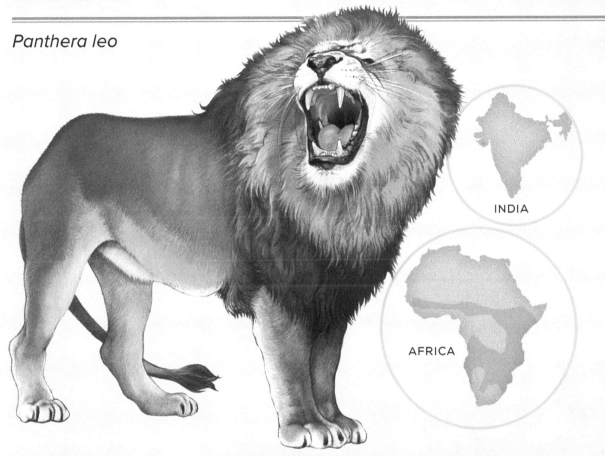

INDIA

AFRICA

## FAST FACTS

**SIZE:** 4.5 to 6.5 feet long; 265 to 420 pounds

**LIFE SPAN:** 12 to 16 years

**FOOD:** Wildebeest, antelopes, and zebras

**SOUNDS:** Purrs, grunts, growls, snarls, hums, puffs, and loud roars

# APPEARANCE

Lions are huge cats! They are a sandy-brown color, the perfect camouflage for stalking through the tall grasses of the savanna. Male lions have large, hairy manes that can be any shade from tan to black. Their manes help them attract mates and look intimidating to other male lions.

Lions can retract their claws, which means that when they aren't using them, the claws are hidden inside sheaths of skin on their paws. This protects the claws and keeps them sharp. When a lion needs to use the claws, special muscles let them extend rapidly.

# SOCIAL STRUCTURE

A pride consists of up to three males, a group of females, and their cubs. Since females tend to stay in the same tribe, they are usually related: sisters, mothers, and grandmothers. Young male lions usually leave the group to start their own pride. They often do this by driving away another male lion from his pride. A male's role is to protect the pride and its territory. The female lions take care of the cubs and hunt for the group.

# RAISING YOUNG

Lionesses give birth away from the pride and usually keep the cubs hidden for the first six weeks of their lives. Cubs are usually around 3 pounds at birth. They nurse from their mother and other females in the pride. A lion baby can be called a cub, a whelp, or a lionet.

# COMMUNICATION

Lions use a variety of sounds to communicate, and each sound has a different meaning. An adult male lion's roar can be heard nearly 5 miles away! This loud roar helps protect the pride's territory by warning intruders to stay away. Lions are social cats that use purring, gentle moans, and huffing and puffing as happy sounds to communicate with others in the pride.

## HUNTING HABITS

Lionesses do most of the hunting for the pride. They hunt in groups for wildebeest, antelopes, and zebras. Using teamwork, they can ambush prey that can typically outrun a single lion. Lions must consume a lot of meat. Females need 11 pounds of meat a day, and males need a whopping 15.4 pounds or more every day!

## SPEED

Lions can run short distances at a top speed of up to 50 miles per hour. They use this short burst of speed to help them capture fast prey. Then they use their strong jaws and retractable claws to finish the job.

## HABITAT

There are two types of lions: African lions and Asiatic lions. The majority of the world's lion population lives in central and southern Africa in territory that consists of grasslands, scrublands, and open woodlands. Asiatic lions live only in India's Gir Forest National Park. This national park includes a deciduous forest, grasslands, scrub jungle, and rocky hills.

## POPULATION

African lions are considered vulnerable and appear on the IUCN. This list keeps track of how severe the risk of extinction is for each of Earth's different animal species. This helps people understand how important it is to protect these animals. The lion population is estimated at 30,000 to 100,000 left in the wild. The Asiatic lions are listed as endangered, with an estimate of only 350 existing lions.

# Snow Leopard

*Panthera uncia*

MOUNTAINS OF CENTRAL ASIA

## - FAST FACTS -

**SIZE:** 4 to 5 feet long; 60 to 120 pounds

**LIFE SPAN:** 10 to 12 years

**FOOD:** Sheep and goats

**SOUNDS:** Purrs, meows, hisses, growls, moans, chuffs, and yowls

## APPEARANCE

Snow leopards are experts at using their camouflage. Their beautiful pale gray fur with blurred black markings helps them blend into the snowy, rocky terrain that they live in. Their fur makes them very hard to see. Their spots become paler in the winter. Large, padded paws help them walk through their snow-covered habitat. Snow leopards also have long tails that let them keep their balance as they climb and jump from rock to rock.

## HABITAT

Snow leopards live in the mountains of central Asia. The snow leopard's habitat extends through Afghanistan, Bhutan, China, India, Kazakhstan, Kyrgyzstan, Mongolia, Nepal, Pakistan, Russia, Tajikistan, and Uzbekistan. They roam some of the world's highest mountains, making it challenging for humans to find and study them.

## RAISING YOUNG

Snow leopards usually have between one and four cubs at a time, and the mother raises them on her own. Since cubs are helpless at birth, they depend on their mother for food and shelter. When the cubs are around 3 months old, they start following their mother to learn important survival skills like hunting. At around 2 years old, the cubs go off on their own.

## SOCIAL STRUCTURE

Snow leopards are solitary cats. They are only found together when mating or when mothers are raising their young. To communicate with other snow leopards or mark their territory, they urinate on the rocks or scratch the terrain.

## HUNTING HABITS

Snow leopards usually eat wild sheep and goats. They are slow eaters and tend to take a few days to consume their prey.

Snow leopards stay near their prey to defend against scavengers such as vultures looking for an easy meal. They are also opportunistic hunters, so snow leopards will eat **domestic** sheep or goats if they are in the area. Snow leopards are rarely aggressive toward humans.

## POPULATION

Since snow leopards are so **elusive**, the exact number that are in the wild is unknown. Experts estimate there are around 4,000 to 6,500 snow leopards, giving them vulnerable status. Due to their beautiful fur, they are in danger of being hunted by poachers. Conservationists are working hard to protect these cats.

# Sunda Clouded Leopard

*Neofelis diardi*

BORNEO

SUMATRA

## - FAST FACTS -

**SIZE:** 27 to 41 inches long; 22 to 55 pounds

**LIFE SPAN:** Up to 17 years

**FOOD:** Monkeys, deer, pigs, and porcupines

**SOUNDS:** Purrs and deep growls

## APPEARANCE

Sunda clouded leopards got their names from the large cloud-shaped blotches on their fur. They have grayish brown to yellowish brown fur under their dark blotches and spots. They have long, slender bodies and long, sharp canine teeth. Their extra-long teeth help them hold onto prey as they climb in trees. Their very long tails help them balance as they climb. Sunda clouded leopards look similar to clouded leopards, but they tend to be slightly darker with more spots filling in their blotches. When compared to the size of their bodies, the canine teeth of Sunda clouded leopards are some of the largest in the cat world!

## HABITAT

These cats are only found on the islands of Borneo and Sumatra in Malaysia. Their habitats include rain forests and hilly mountains. They spend a lot of time lying on a branch up in a tree.

## HISTORY

Sunda clouded leopards were identified as a separate species from the mainland clouded leopards in 2006. After running tests, scientists found that they were each their own unique species and had separated about 2 million years ago!

## BEHAVIOR

Not a lot is known about these big cats' behavior in the wild. They are very secretive and elusive. They are great climbers and spend a lot of time in trees. They have flexible ankle joints that allow them to climb down a tree headfirst.

## RAISING YOUNG

Sunda clouded leopards are solitary unless they are mating or females are raising their cubs. Female Sunda clouded leopards can have from one to five cubs in a litter, with an average of two cubs per litter. Mothers nurse their cubs and teach them to hunt.

Cubs become independent at about 10 months old and go off on their own.

## HUNTING HABITS

Sunda clouded leopards hunt a variety of animals including monkeys, deer, pigs, and porcupines. They hunt on land and in trees. They are ambush hunters and drop down upon unsuspecting prey from a tree.

## POPULATION

The Sunda clouded leopard population is considered vulnerable and at risk for extinction. The islands that they live on have experienced deforestation in recent years which is destroying the leopards' environment and causing habitat loss.

# Tiger

*Panthera tigris*

ASIA

## FAST FACTS

**SIZE:** Up to 10 feet long; 220 to 660 pounds

**LIFE SPAN:** 10 to 15 years

**FOOD:** Pigs, deer, water buffalo, and crocodiles

**SOUNDS:** Roars, growls, chuffs, hisses, and moans

## APPEARANCE

Most tigers have orangish fur with dark stripes. A tiger's stripes vary from light brown to black. No two tigers have identical stripes; they all have a unique pattern, like human fingerprints. The stripes give tigers camouflage with their surroundings. Researchers also use the different stripe patterns to identify specific tigers in the wild. Tigers are the largest cats in the world and have strong jaws and sharp canine teeth for hunting large animals.

## PARTICULAR SKILLS

Unlike many cats, tigers are great swimmers and relax in water to cool off. Tigers can jump forward up to 30 feet; their leaping ability helps when they are ambushing prey.

## RAISING YOUNG

Tigers are mostly solitary, which means they are often found alone. The only time tigers spend time together is when they are mating or raising young. Female tigers give birth to up to seven cubs at a time. The average number of cubs per litter is between two and four. The cubs usually weigh a little over 2 pounds and are completely dependent on their mother at birth. They stay with their mother for about 2 years until they can successfully hunt on their own.

## COMMUNICATION

Even though tigers are solitary animals, communication is still important. A tiger's loud roar can be heard from about 2 miles away! They use sounds to communicate, and they also use signals and markings to claim their territory. Tigers are extremely territorial, so being able to identify their territory is very important. They mark their territory by scratching trees or urinating.

## POPULATION

Tigers are considered critically endangered. There are only about 3,900 tigers left in the wild. Tigers used to roam a large portion of Asia. Now they are limited to about 7 percent of their former range, due to habitat loss and hunting.

## HABITAT

Tigers can be found in parts of south and Southeast Asia, China, and eastern Russia. They live in temperate forests, evergreen forests, tropical rain forests, mangrove swamps, grasslands, and savannas.

## HUNTING HABITS

Tigers typically hunt at night, sneaking up on prey and biting the back of the animal's head or neck with their powerful jaws. They are also opportunistic hunters, which means if prey walks by them during the day, tigers will pounce and take advantage of the opportunity for an extra meal. They usually hunt large animals like pigs, deer, water buffalo, and even crocodiles. Tigers can eat up to 88 pounds of meat in a single day!

Lion

# THE SMALL CATS

There are many different species of small wild cats. Scientists spend a lot of time studying these cats and separating them into different species based on their characteristics and genetics. Scientists watch the cats' behavior and study their bones and DNA. Scientists give small cats scientific names that are recognized by other scientists around the world, no matter what language they speak. The cats have common names, too, but those differ from one language to another, which is why scientists use a name that the whole world recognizes for each type of animal. Scientists are constantly obtaining new information to determine the number of species and subspecies of cats there are in the world.

In this chapter, you will learn about 28 different species of small cats and get to read about their many skills and adaptations. These cats range in size, color, shape, and patterns. One thing they all have in common is that they are all carnivores. These cats are fierce hunters and catch their prey in trees, in water, by digging underground, and even by leaping high into the air! They live in a variety of habitats all over the world.

# African Golden Cat

*Caracal aurata*

AFRICA

## FAST FACTS

**SIZE:** 24 to 37 inches long; 24 to 30 pounds

**LIFE SPAN:** Up to 12 years (in captivity)

**FOOD:** Rodents, small antelope, birds, bats, and primates

**SOUNDS:** Meows, growls, and hisses

## APPEARANCE

African golden cats get their name from the reddish-gold color of their fur. Some African golden cats are grayish or even have darker coats. The coats on these cats vary in more than just color. Some African golden cats have spots while others do not. Most of them have white bellies with large dark spots. They have short legs and rounded ears and are about double the size of a house cat.

## HABITAT

African golden cats live in tropical rain forests along the equatorial line in Africa. They prefer dense forests with little human activity.

## BEHAVIOR

Scientists have set up cameras to try to study more about the behavior of African golden cats. From their observations, they have seen that the cats are active at all different times of the day and that they are solitary cats that live alone.

## RAISING YOUNG

Very little is known about how African golden cats raise their young in the wild. But based on observations of those in captivity, they have two cubs at a time.

## HUNTING HABITS

It is thought that African golden cats do most of their hunting with the stalk-and-rush technique while hunting on the ground. They eat rodents, small antelope, birds, bats, and primates.

## POPULATION

The exact population of African golden cats is unknown, but they are listed as vulnerable on the IUCN. Habitat loss, hunting, and being leopards' prey are some of the major threats this cat faces. Some tribes use the tail of the African golden cat as a symbol of good luck on their elephant hunts.

# Andean Mountain Cat

*Leopardus jacobita*

THE ANDES MOUNTAINS
IN SOUTH AMERICA

## FAST FACTS

**SIZE:** 22 to 25 inches long; 8 to 13 pounds

**LIFE SPAN:** Unknown

**FOOD:** Chinchillas, mountain vizcachas, reptiles, and birds

**SOUNDS:** Meows, growls, purrs, and screams

## APPEARANCE

Andean mountain cats are mostly gray or silver with rust-colored spots on their body and dark stripes on their legs. They have long bushy tails with dark rings around them. Andean mountain cats have thick fur that helps them blend in with their rocky habitat.

## PARTICULAR SKILLS

Andean mountain cats have extremely long tails. They use their long tails to help them balance as they chase prey that switches directions a lot through rough terrain. They usually hold their tail up high when on the hunt.

## HABITAT

Andean mountain cats live in rocky areas, shrubland, and grassland habitats. They live in Argentina, Bolivia, Chile, and Peru. Most Andean mountain cats are found living above the timberline. They live in remote, mountainous regions, which makes studying them more difficult. There are no known Andean mountain cats in captivity.

## RAISING YOUNG

Very little is known about the reproduction of these cats. Estimated litter sizes are between one and three kittens.

## HUNTING HABITS

Andean mountain cats hunt chinchillas, mountain vizcachas, reptiles, birds, and other small mammals. They are agile hunters that can navigate tough terrain while chasing a meal.

## POPULATION

Andean mountain cats are an endangered species with only an estimated 1,378 adults living in the wild. They are one of the rarest cats in the world.

# Asian Golden Cat

*Catopuma temminckii*

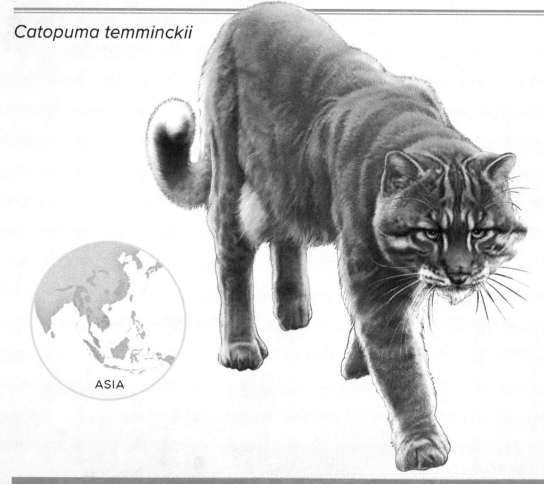

ASIA

## FAST FACTS

**SIZE:** 26 to 41 inches long; up to 33 pounds

**LIFE SPAN:** Up to 20 years (in captivity)

**FOOD:** Lizards, squirrels, small snakes, rodents, and birds

**SOUNDS:** Purrs, meows, hisses, and growls

## APPEARANCE

Asian golden cats are strong, medium-sized cats that have a variety of fur colors. Their coats can be fox-red, gold, brown, black, or gray. The fur on their bellies is usually white. They can have white and black lines on the fur on their face.

## BEHAVIOR

Even though they are good climbers, they spend most of their time on the ground. It is thought that Asian golden cats are solitary like most other wild cats. Camera traps set up by scientists are used to try to capture more information about these cats since not much is known about their behavior.

## RAISING YOUNG

Asian golden cats have between one and four kittens in each litter. The kittens are a tiny 9 ounces when they are born, but they grow quickly. Kittens stay with their mother until they are around a year old.

## HABITAT

Asian golden cats live in forests, grasslands, savannas, and shrubland habitats throughout different parts of Asia.

## HUNTING HABITS

Asian golden cats are carnivores who eat lizards, squirrels, small snakes, rodents, and birds. In some areas they also hunt larger animals like wild pigs and small deer.

## POPULATION

There is no exact estimate for how many Asian golden cats are left in the wild, but they are considered near threatened and are at risk of extinction. The population is decreasing because of deforestation and human hunting.

# Black-footed Cat

*Felis nigripes*

AFRICA

## FAST FACTS

**SIZE:** 14 to 20 inches long;
2.4 to 4.2 pounds

**LIFE SPAN:** 6.5 years

**FOOD:** Rodents, lizards, insects,
and birds

**SOUNDS:** Purrs, gurgles, hisses,
and growls

## APPEARANCE

Black-footed cats got their name from the black pads on the bottom of their paws. They have tan fur with black spots, a round head, and big eyes. At first glance, you would never guess these cats were fierce hunters. Their tiny size and big eyes make them look more like a child's favorite stuffed animal than deadly cats.

## RAISING YOUNG

Black-footed cats are solitary except for mating and when females raise their kittens. Females usually have two kittens per litter. These kittens only weigh 2 to 3 ounces when they are born. Mothers give birth in a den or burrow. They frequently move to different burrows, probably to avoid predators. The babies rely on their mom completely for the first few months, then go off on their own. The kittens stay within the range of their mother for the first few days they are on their own.

## HABITAT

Black-footed cats live in Botswana, Namibia, and South Africa. Their habitat includes grasslands, savannas, and deserts. They use other animals' **abandoned** burrows or termite mounds for shelter. Since they are so small, it is easy for them to stay hidden in the tall grass while hunting rodents and other small creatures.

## PARTICULAR SKILLS

Black-footed cats have excellent night vision and use their large eyes to watch for prey in the dark. They also have great hearing and can sense the tiniest sounds of other creatures that are about to become their next meal.

## HUNTING HABITS

Although they weigh less than 5 pounds, these fierce cats average 10 to 14 kills a night! Black-footed cats are great hunters and are successful on about 60 percent of their hunting attempts. They eat rodents, lizards, insects, and birds. Black-footed cats aren't a threat to large animals, but because of the number of successful kills they make each night, these cats are known as the deadliest cats in the world. Black-footed cats are nocturnal, doing most of their hunting after dark.

## POPULATION

Black-footed cats are considered vulnerable, with an estimated 9,707 adults left in the wild.

# Bobcat

*Lynx rufus*

NORTH
AMERICA

## FAST FACTS

**SIZE:** 26 to 41 inches long; 11 to 30 pounds

**LIFE SPAN:** 10 to 12 years

**FOOD:** Mice, squirrels, lizards, snakes, and even small deer

**SOUNDS:** Chortles, chirps, and screams

# APPEARANCE

Bobcats are about twice the size of a house cat. Bobcats get their name from their stubby tails. Most cats have long tails, but bobcats look as though their tails have been cut off or "bobbed." Bobcats often have spotted fur that ranges from brownish to gray. Their ears have a tuft of fur at the tips. Their long whiskers help them feel to make sure they can fit through small spaces.

# BEHAVIOR

Bobcats are solitary cats. They tell other bobcats to stay away by marking their territory with smells. They spend most of their lives alone, searching for their next meal.

# RAISING YOUNG

Female bobcats have their kittens in a shelter such as a hollow tree, cave, or in thick shrubs. They have one to six kittens at a time. The kittens stay with their mother for up to a year while they learn how to hunt and take care of themselves. At about a year old, the bobcat kittens go off on their own.

# PARTICULAR SKILLS

Bobcats are superfast! They can run at speeds up to 30 miles per hour. They can leap up to 12 feet, which is a skill that comes in handy when bobcats are trying to catch their prey. They are also excellent swimmers! Bobcats have keen night vision, which helps when they are hunting in low light.

# HUNTING HABITS

Bobcats eat small animals and rodents like hares, mice, squirrels, lizards, and snakes. But sometimes they also capture small deer. They stalk their prey, then attack fiercely with a quick pounce. They travel up to 7 miles during a hunt.

# HABITAT

Bobcats sleep in hollowed-out trees or small caves that provide shelter from the weather. They live throughout North America in the mountains, forests, swamps, and deserts. Because bobcats adapt to many different environments, they are the most common wild cat in the United States.

## POPULATION

Even though they stay out of sight, there are plenty of bobcats in North America. Experts estimate that there are nearly 1 million bobcats remaining in the wild.

# Borneo Bay Cat

*Catopuma badia*

ISLAND
OF BORNEO

## FAST FACTS

**SIZE:** 21 to 27 inches long; 6 to 9 pounds

**LIFE SPAN:** Unknown

**FOOD:** Rodents and small animals

**SOUNDS:** Growls and hisses

## APPEARANCE

Borneo bay cats are about the size of a large house cat. They have long, slender bodies and very long tails. They can be a reddish-brown or a gray color with a white belly. They have round faces and small, rounded ears.

## BEHAVIOR

Borneo bay cats are among the rarest and least-studied cats in the world. Barely any information is known about their behavior. Researchers have set up camera traps to try to learn more about these rare cats. They believe they are probably solitary cats because they have only been seen alone in the videos captured. There are no Borneo bay cats in captivity for scientists to study.

## RAISING YOUNG

No one knows how Borneo bay cats raise their young since this has never been observed in the wild or in captivity.

## HISTORY

Until 1992, a live Borneo bay cat had never been studied. When a female Borneo bay cat was captured and brought to a museum, researchers were able to get blood samples for the first time and make observations about the size and appearance of the cat. The cat was in poor health and died after a short time, so researchers were unable to observe its behaviors.

## HABITAT

Borneo bay cats are only found on the island of Borneo. They live in dense forests and probably feed on rodents and small animals.

## POPULATION

These cats are very rare. Although the exact number in the wild is unknown, they are considered endangered. Researchers are trying to learn more about Borneo bay cats so they can protect them and the environment necessary for their survival.

# Canada Lynx

*Lynx canadensis*

CANADA AND
NORTHERN US

## FAST FACTS

**SIZE:** 30 to 42 inches long;
11 to 37 pounds

**FOOD:** Mostly snowshoe hares,
sometimes rodents and fish

**LIFE SPAN:** About 15 years

**SOUNDS:** Meows, hisses,
and purrs

## APPEARANCE

Canada lynx are medium-sized cats with black tufts of hair above each ear. They have thick hair on the sides of their faces. This makes their faces look wider than they are. They have long legs and short stubby tails. The ends of their tails look as if they were dipped into black paint. Their fur color changes with the season. During the summer it is a reddish brown, which then changes into a thick gray coat for the winter. The coat color change helps them blend in with their environment based on the season.

## HABITAT

Canada lynx live throughout most of Canada. They can also be found in Alaska and in some parts of the continental United States. They thrive in cold environments in forests, shrubland, and grasslands.

## BEHAVIOR

Canada lynx are solitary cats. They are only found together to mate or when females are raising kittens. They often hunt at night and times when their prey is most active.

## RAISING YOUNG

Canada lynx can have up to eight kittens per litter. The kittens typically stay with their mother for at least 10 months. The litter sizes are larger during times when the snowshoe hare population is bigger.

## PARTICULAR SKILLS

Canada lynx have huge paws that work like snowshoes, which allow them to walk on deep snow without sinking. They have excellent vision and use it to spot their prey from far distances.

## HUNTING HABITS

The Canada lynx's primary food source is snowshoe hares. Scientists have noticed an increase in the Canada lynx population when the population of snowshoe hares rises. Canada lynx are ambush hunters and wait for the opportunity to pounce on their prey. When snowshoe hares are scarce, they will eat rodents, fish, and other small animals.

## POPULATION

The population of Canada lynx is stable. The biggest threat to their population is habitat loss. Hunting these cats is legal in Canada and Alaska, and they are often trapped for their fur.

# Caracal

*Caracal caracal*

AFRICA,
THE MIDDLE EAST,
AND INDIA

## FAST FACTS

**SIZE:** 24 to 42 inches long;
13 to 44 pounds

**FOOD:** Monkeys, rodents,
and mongooses

**LIFE SPAN:** About 12 years

**SOUNDS:** Meows, cries, snarls,
hisses, and growls

## APPEARANCE

Wondering where these cats got their name? The word "caracal" comes from a Turkish word that means "black-eared." They have large pointed ears with long black tufts of hair on the tip of each ear. Their slender bodies are covered with reddish-gold fur.

## HABITAT

Caracals do well in the dry climates of Africa and from the Middle East to India. They can be found in savanna, forest, grassland, shrub-land, and desert habitats.

## PARTICULAR SKILLS

Caracals have strong back legs that help give them high vertical leaps. They can jump up to 10 feet high and are able to swat birds out of the air! Caracals also keep their claws very sharp, which helps in hunting and climbing trees.

Caracals can run very fast. Special footpads muffle the noise from their feet so they can sneak up on prey.

## BEHAVIOR

Caracals are solitary cats and spend most of their adult lives alone. They mark their territory with scratches and scents.

## RAISING YOUNG

Caracal mothers have between one and four kittens in each litter. They have their kittens in other animals' abandoned dens. It takes about 10 days for the kittens to open their eyes after they are born. Kittens can start eating meat at only 2 months old. The kittens stay with their mothers for up to a year while they learn how to hunt. Caracal mothers have been seen snuggling with their kittens, show-ing these fierce hunters have a softer side.

## HUNTING HABITS

Caracals are carnivores and only eat meat. They hunt mostly at night and are not picky about what type of prey they eat. Caracals will eat any animal that they can catch, including monkeys, rodents, mongooses, and sometimes even antelopes.

## POPULATION

The caracal population is currently stable, and they are not at risk for extinction.

# Chinese Mountain Cat

*Felis bieti*

CHINA

## FAST FACTS

**SIZE:** 27 to 33 inches long; 10 to 20 pounds

**LIFE SPAN:** Unknown

**FOOD:** Rodents, **pikas**, **voles**, other small mammals, and birds

**SOUNDS:** Unknown

## APPEARANCE

Chinese mountain cats are slightly larger than house cats. Their thick, fluffy fur color changes slightly with the seasons. In the summer, their fur has a brownish color, and in the winter, it turns a yellowish gray. Their tails have dark rings around them and usually have dark tips. Their ears have short tufts of fur on the tips.

## HABITAT

Chinese mountain cats are only found in China. They are mainly found in the mountains and high elevation grasslands. Their thick fur helps protect them from the harsh mountain weather. They are sometimes called "Chinese desert cats" even though they are not known to live in any deserts.

## BEHAVIOR

There are no Chinese mountain cats in captivity, and very few studies have been done on them in the wild. As a result, there is very little information on their behavior. They seem to be solitary cats except while breeding or raising young. They rest in burrows during the day and are thought to be most active at night.

## RAISING YOUNG

Chinese mountain cats usually have two to four kittens at a time. The mothers have their kittens in a burrow. Mothers care for the kittens until the kittens are ready to be independent at around 7 or 8 months old.

## HUNTING HABITS

Chinese mountain cats use their excellent hearing to listen for prey running in underground tunnels. The Chinese mountain cats quickly dig them out. Their diet consists of rodents, pikas, voles, other small mammals, and sometimes birds.

## POPULATION

There are fewer than 10,000 estimated Chinese mountain cats remaining in the wild. A big threat to the cats' population is the shrinking population of its main food source. People view pikas and the other rodents these cats eat as pests. When people poison the rodents, it decreases the amount of available prey for these rare cats. And if they eat the poisoned rodents, the Chinese mountain cats are also poisoned.

# Eurasian Lynx

*Lynx lynx*

EUROPE, RUSSIA, AND CENTRAL ASIA

## FAST FACTS

**SIZE:** 31 to 43 inches long; 33 to 64 pounds

**LIFE SPAN:** Up to 17 years

**FOOD:** Deer, hares, foxes, and rodents

**SOUNDS:** Growls, coughs, grunts, meows, hisses, purrs, and chatters

## APPEARANCE

Eurasian lynx are the largest in the lynx family. They have mostly yellowish to brownish gray fur with white fur on their bellies. They often have darker spots or markings on their fur. They have dark tufts of hair that stick out at the tips of their ears. Their faces have a ruff of hair, almost like a beard, that makes their faces appear wider than they are. Eurasian lynx have short tails with black tips. They have long legs with wide paws that work like snowshoes, helping them walk on deep snow.

## HABITAT

Eurasian lynx can be found across much of Europe, Russia, and Asia. They have one of the largest ranges of any wild cat, living in both dense forests and rocky areas. Their fur is thick to protect them from the cold weather that they encounter in their habitat.

## BEHAVIOR

Eurasian lynx are secretive cats and prefer to stay out of sight. They live in thick forests with plenty of hiding places. They spend most of their adult lives alone. They are only seen together to mate or when females are raising kittens. They communicate with other cats through scents and sounds.

## RAISING YOUNG

Eurasian lynx females will find a den and line it with soft items like fur, feathers, or grass for added comfort for their kittens. Mothers will usually have two or three kittens in a litter. The babies depend on their mothers completely at birth. At 6 weeks old, the kittens start learning how to hunt.

## HUNTING HABITS

Eurasian lynx are the third-largest predator in Europe. Only the brown bear and wolf are bigger.

Eurasian lynx prefer large prey such as deer. If large prey is hard to find, they will eat hares, foxes, rodents, and birds. They usually use the stalk-and-pounce method for hunting, surprising their prey with a sneak attack. They are so strong that they can bring down prey larger than themselves. They are mostly active during dawn, dusk, and after dark.

## PARTICULAR SKILLS

Eurasian lynx are good swimmers and have been seen swimming across rivers. They are also excellent climbers and can be found relaxing in trees or climbing trees in order to drop down on their prey. They have superb eyesight that helps them spot their prey from a distance.

## POPULATION

The population of Eurasian lynx is currently stable. The population throughout Europe is fragmented, or separated, due to habitat loss. The largest population of these cats is found in Russia and China.

# Fishing Cat

*Prionailurus viverrinus*

SOUTH AND
SOUTHEAST ASIA

## FAST FACTS

**SIZE:** 22 to 45 inches long;
11 to 31 pounds

**FOOD:** Fish, crustaceans, frogs,
snakes, and ducks

**LIFE SPAN:** 10 to 12 years

**SOUNDS:** Hisses, growls, meows,
and chitters

## APPEARANCE

Fishing cats are gray and brown with dark spots and stripes along their backs. These cats have many features that make them strong swimmers. They have webbed front feet with sharp claws. Their claws cannot be fully retracted, which means they are always sticking out a little bit. They have strong bodies and short tails. Their special fur keeps them warm even when they get wet, and their fur pattern camouflages them in their environment.

## HABITAT

These cats live in South and Southeast Asia. They live in wetlands, marshes, swamps, and mangrove forests. They prefer areas near water and can often be found near rivers, streams, and standing water.

## BEHAVIOR

These cats have been seen "fishing" in shallow water by reaching in and scooping up the fish with their sharp claws. They will also dive under the water to catch fish and other aquatic animals. They aren't picky eaters and capture whatever is available. There have even been reports of a fishing cat sneakily diving underwater to grab a duck by its feet!

## RAISING YOUNG

Females give birth to their kittens in a den. Fishing cats have one to four kittens in each litter. The kittens learn how to fish and hunt by watching their mother. By around 10 months old, the kittens will be able to hunt and live on their own.

## PARTICULAR SKILLS

Fishing cats are built for their environment and have webbing between their toes to help them swim and walk through the mud without sinking. They also have sharp claws that help them grasp their prey. They have two layers of fur. One layer is shorter and keeps the cat warm and dry after spending time in the water. The second layer is longer and provides the fur color that helps these cats blend in with their surroundings.

## HUNTING HABITS

Most of the fishing cats' diet is fish. They also eat other aquatic animals like crustaceans, frogs, snakes, and ducks. Sometimes they eat rodents and wild pigs.

## POPULATION

The fishing cat population is considered vulnerable due to the loss of its habitat. As more humans populate the earth, they take over more land. This means the wetland habitat that fishing cats prefer is shrinking. Humans are the only known predator for fishing cats.

# Flat-headed Cat

*Prionailurus planiceps*

SOUTHEAST
ASIA

## FAST FACTS

**SIZE:** 13 to 20 inches long;
3 to 6 pounds

**LIFE SPAN:** Unknown in the wild;
up to 14 years in captivity

**FOOD:** Fish, crabs, small rodents,
and frogs

**SOUNDS:** Purrs and other short-
range sounds

## APPEARANCE

Flat-headed cats get their name from their flat forehead. They are about the same size as a house cat. They have large brown eyes that are very close together. They have small rounded ears and short tails. Flat-headed cats have thick reddish-brown to dark brown fur. They have webbed toes on their paws, which allow them to swim. They also have sharp claws that don't fully retract. They have long, narrow jaws, and teeth that point backward to keep slippery fish and frogs from slipping out of their mouth.

## HABITAT

These cats are very elusive, which means that they are very rarely seen and studied by people. Their habitats are lowland forests, mangroves, and swamp forests. Many of the sightings of these cats occur along bodies of water. They have been found in various parts of Southeast Asia.

## BEHAVIOR

Very little is known about flat-headed cats' behavior because they are so rare. They are thought to be mostly nocturnal and active during early morning hours. Flat-headed cats "wash" objects in water with their paws, much like a raccoon would do. In captivity they appear to prefer the water to land.

## HUNTING HABITS

These cats eat fish, crabs, small rodents, and frogs. To catch fish, they will put their head completely underwater to bite fish. Their backward-facing teeth hold the wriggling fish in their mouth. They take the fish onto shore before eating it. This way the fish can't easily escape into the water.

## POPULATION

Flat-headed cats are very rare, and it is estimated that there are fewer than 2,500 of these cats in the wild. The biggest threats to these endangered cats are habitat loss and water pollution.

# Geoffroy's Cat

*Leopardus geoffroyi*

ARGENTINA,
BOLIVIA, BRAZIL,
CHILE, PARAGUAY,
AND URUGUAY

## FAST FACTS

**SIZE:** 17 to 34 inches long;
6 to 13 pounds

**LIFE SPAN:** Up to 18 years

**FOOD:** Rodents, rabbits, birds,
fish, reptiles, and small mammals

**SOUNDS:** Purrs, hisses, snarls,
calls, and growls

## APPEARANCE

These small cats are about the same size as a house cat. They have a spotted fur coat with a base color of either yellowish brown or grayish silver. They can have a variety of black stripes and markings on their body in addition to their spots. Their tails have dark rings. Some of these cats have spots that are nearly impossible to see because their base fur color is so dark.

## HABITAT

These cats live in South America. They can be found in the Andes Mountain range in southern Bolivia, southern Brazil, Paraguay, Argentina, Uruguay, and southern Chile. Their habitat includes grasslands, forests, and marshes. They prefer thick vegetation which offers shelter and allows them to hide from prey.

## HISTORY

Geoffroy's cats got their name from French naturalist Geoffroy Saint-Hilaire. He identified the cat as its own species. He discovered them during his travels to South America in the nineteenth century.

## BEHAVIOR

Geoffroy's cats are mostly solitary unless they are looking for a mate or are mothers raising their kittens. They are nocturnal and do most of their hunting after dark or at dawn and dusk. These cats are great swimmers. They are also excellent climbers and can easily walk along tree branches.

## RAISING YOUNG

Mothers have between one and four kittens in each litter. They give birth in a den. The den can be between rocks, hidden in thick brush, or in the hollow of a tree. Kittens only weigh a few ounces when they are born, blind and helpless. After a couple of weeks, the kittens learn to open their eyes and walk. Kittens stay with their mother for about 8 months while learning the skills that they will need to be independent.

## HUNTING HABITS

Geoffroy's cats control the rodent population. They also eat rabbits, birds, fish, reptiles, and small mammals. They are generalist hunters and catch whatever small animals are available in their area. Even though these cats do most of their hunting on land, they can also hunt in the water and while climbing in trees.

## POPULATION

The population of Geoffroy's cats is healthy and widespread. Predators of these cats include domestic dogs, humans, and occasionally pumas. One threat to the Geoffroy's cat population is habitat loss due to deforestation.

# Iberian Lynx

*Lynx pardinus*

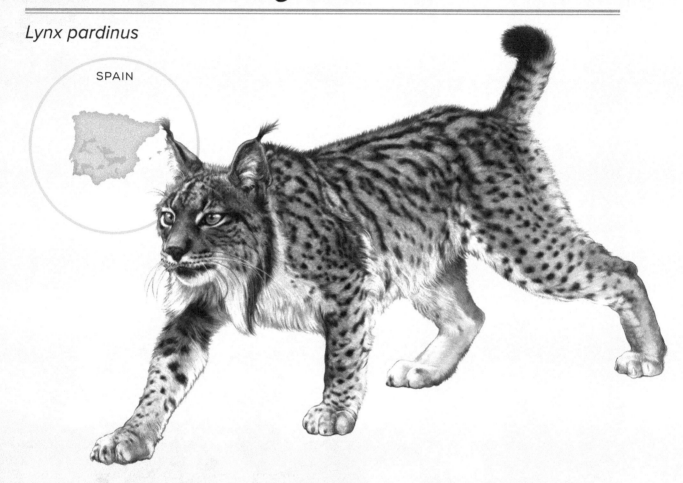

SPAIN

## FAST FACTS

**SIZE:** 27 to 32 inches long; 15 to 22 pounds

**FOOD:** Mostly rabbits, but also ducks, small deer, and birds

**LIFE SPAN:** Up to 13 years

**SOUNDS:** Puffs when irritated

## APPEARANCE

Iberian lynx are smaller than the Eurasian lynx. They have black spots and tawny-colored fur. They have black tufts of fur that stick up from their ears and a ruff of fur like a beard around their faces. Their short tails have black tips.

## HABITAT

The Iberian lynx used to have a large range, but in recent years they have only been found in a few areas in Spain. Conservation-ists have started to reintroduce captive Iberian lynx to the wild and have begun to add some back into Portugal as well. These cats prefer Mediterranean woodland and shrubland habitats that have a large supply of their favorite food, rabbits.

## BEHAVIOR

They are mostly active when their prey is active. They are mainly nocturnal and also hunt at dusk and dawn. Iberian lynx are solitary cats unless they are mating or females raising young.

## RAISING YOUNG

Iberian lynx mothers have between one and four kittens in each litter. Most choose to have their babies in the shelter of a hollow or hollowed-out tree. Kittens will nurse from their mothers for 3 or 4 months. By 28 days old, kittens can start eating meat. The kittens become independent around 10 months old, but they may stay within their mother's territory until they reach 20 months of age.

## HUNTING HABITS

Iberian lynx mostly eat rabbits. When hunting rabbits, they bite their skull to capture prey. If rab-bits aren't available, they will eat ducks, small deer, or birds. An adult lynx needs to eat about one rabbit every day. A mother raising her young needs to catch about 3 rabbits a day. If the lynx have extra food, they may bury their leftovers and come back to eat them at another time.

## PARTICULAR SKILLS

Iberian lynx have keen vision. They also have excellent hearing. Iberian lynx have large furry paws that help them walk quietly on the snow. The paws also help them regulate their body temperatures in cold weather.

## POPULATION

The population of Iberian lynx is one of the most endangered in the world. In 2002, the population dropped below 100 adults in the wild. Luckily, conservationists are working to increase the population. Conservationists set up camera traps to closely watch the Iberian lynx. By keeping a close eye on them, they can learn how to better protect the population so that these cats do not become extinct. Threats to these cats include loss of prey, habitat loss, human traps, and road accidents.

# Jaguarundi

*Herpailurus yagouaroundi*

NORTH AMERICA
AND
SOUTH AMERICA

## FAST FACTS

**SIZE:** 21 to 30 inches long;
6 to 15 pounds

**LIFE SPAN:** Up to 15 years

**FOOD:** Rodents, rabbits,
armadillos, opossums, quail, wild
turkey, reptiles, frogs, fish, and
domestic poultry

**SOUNDS:** Chirps, purrs, chatters,
yaps, whistles, and screams

## APPEARANCE

These unique-looking cats have small, flattened heads and long, skinny bodies. Their fur can range from brown, black, and gray to a tawny yellow or reddish shade.

## HABITAT

Jaguarundi prefer habitats that have dense floor vegetation. They are found in dry scrub, swamp, savanna, woodland, and forest habitats. Starting from southern Texas all the way to northern Argentina, jaguarundi have a huge range from North America to South America.

## BEHAVIOR

Jaguarundi can jump, climb, and swim. Unlike many cats, jaguarundi tend to be active during the day. They were once thought to be solitary, like most cats, but recently some jaguarundi have been spotted traveling in pairs. Jaguarundi are shy and elusive cats, but because they are more active during the day, people notice them.

## COMMUNICATION

Jaguarundi are very vocal cats and can make 13 different calls. Some of the sounds they can make are chirps, purrs, chatters, yaps, whistles, and screams. To ward off intruders in their territory, they hiss or spit. Mother cats purr at their kittens, and they respond with a series of short peeps.

## RAISING YOUNG

Females have their babies in dens within thick vegetation or hollow logs. Jaguarundi have between one and four kittens in each litter. When kittens are born, they have spots on their fur, but those spots fade as they get older. Kittens will nurse for about 2 months, then they begin to follow their mothers. At around 10 months old, they go off on their own.

## PARTICULAR SKILLS

Jaguarundi spend most of their time on land, but they are great swimmers. They also have long tails that help them balance as they climb trees and leap from one tree branch to another. They can also jump around 6 feet into the air, which is as high as an adult human standing up. They jump to snatch birds from the air.

## HUNTING HABITS

The jaguarundis' diet consists of rodents, rabbits, armadillos, opossums, quail, wild turkey, reptiles, frogs, fish, and domestic poultry. Because they sometimes attack domestic poultry, farmers may kill them.

## POPULATION

The population of jaguarundi is not currently considered at risk for extinction. But even though it isn't endangered, the population is declining because of habitat loss. Expanding cities and deforestation are reducing their natural habitat.

# Jungle Cat

*Felis chaus*

ASIA
AND AFRICA

## FAST FACTS

**SIZE:** 23 to 30 inches long;
11 to 20 pounds

**LIFE SPAN:** Up to 15 years
(in captivity)

**FOOD:** Rodents, lizards, frogs,
birds, rabbits, snakes, and
occasionally fruit

**SOUNDS:** Meows, chirps, purrs,
growls, gurgles, hisses, and barks

## APPEARANCE

Jungle cats have a mostly plain coat with light brown stripes on their legs and rings on their tails. Their fur can be sandy yellow, reddish, or gray. They have long, slender bodies and small heads. Their large, triangular ears are close together on the top of their heads.

## HABITAT

Jungle cats live in India, Egypt, west and central Asia, south Asia, Sri Lanka, and Southeast Asia. Jungle cats prefer to live in environments with dense vegetation, but they are also found in desert, woodland, grassland, and deciduous forest habitats. Even though they are named jungle cats, they are not found in rain forests. People call them "reed cats" or "swamp cats" because tall reeds and grasses are a common habitat for them.

## RAISING YOUNG

Female jungle cats have between one and six kittens in each litter. They have their kittens in dens within dense stands of reeds, hollow or hollowed-out trees, or other animals' abandoned burrows. When jungle cat kittens are born, they have dark stripes that fade as they grow. At around 6 months old, kittens begin catching their own prey. They become independent around 8 or 9 months old.

## HISTORY

Drawings of jungle cats have been found in ancient Egyptian art. Some jungle cats were mummified, and their remains have been found in Egyptian tombs.

## PARTICULAR SKILLS

Jungle cats are great climbers. They have claws on all of their paws that help them climb up and down trees. They are also good swimmers. Jungle cats use their large ears to listen for prey. Their excellent hearing helps them pinpoint their next meal.

## HUNTING HABITS

The jungle cat is active mostly in the early morning to late afternoon. Jungle cats eat rodents, lizards, frogs, birds, rabbits, snakes, and occasionally fruit. The jungle cat hunts its prey by stalking and pouncing on it. They have also been seen leaping into the air to catch birds.

## POPULATION

The world's population of jungle cats is not at risk for extinction. However, the population is decreasing because of habitat loss, poisoning, and trapping.

# Kodkod

*Leopardus guigna*

ARGENTINA
AND CHILE

## FAST FACTS

**SIZE:** 14 to 20 inches long;
3.3 to 6.6 pounds

**FOOD:** Rodents, birds, reptiles,
and large insects

**LIFE SPAN:** Up to 11 years
(in captivity)

**SOUNDS:** Unknown

## APPEARANCE

Kodkods are also commonly known as Chilean cats, guiñas, or guignas. They are the smallest wild cats in the Americas and do not grow larger than a house cat. They have grayish to brown fur with small black spots and stripes all over their bodies. They have short, thick tails. Some completely dark kodkods have spots that are only visible in bright light. Their fur gives them camouflage in trees or in the vegetation on the forest floor. They have large footpads that help them climb.

## HABITAT

Kodkods are only found in Chile and western Argentina. They spend their time in trees and on land in moist temperate forests. They are often found in areas with extremely thick bamboo. They like to live where there is thick ground cover.

## RAISING YOUNG

Kodkods are rare cats, and very little is known about how they raise their young in the wild. Kodkod mothers have between one and four kittens per litter. Unlike many cats, kodkods are 2 years old before they can have kittens.

## BEHAVIOR

Since these cats are so rare and secretive, there isn't a lot of information about their behavior and communication. These solitary cats hide in trees and in thick ground vegetation. They appear to be active during the day and the night.

## PARTICULAR SKILLS

Kodkods are excellent climbers and climb trees for shelter or to hide from predators. They also keep an eye out for possible prey from a high perch in a tree. Like many other types of cats, kodkods have excellent sight, smell, and hearing. Their superb senses help them to be successful hunters.

## HUNTING HABITS

Kodkods eat rodents, birds, reptiles, and large insects. Kodkods sometimes raid bird nests in trees. At times they eat chickens and geese, and farmers sometimes kill kodkods in order to protect their poultry.

## POPULATION

The exact number of kodkods is unknown. The threats to their survival include habitat loss, humans, and domestic dogs. Since they have such a small range, keeping their habitat stable is very important to their survival.

# Leopard Cat

*Prionailurus bengalensis*

ASIA

## FAST FACTS

**SIZE:** 18 to 29 inches long; 4 to 15 pounds

**LIFE SPAN:** Up to 15 years (in captivity)

**FOOD:** Mice, rats, birds, amphibians, lizards, and insects

**SOUNDS:** Purrs and cries (sound much like a house cat)

## APPEARANCE

Leopard cats are about the same size as domestic cats, although they have longer legs. They get their name from the leopard-like spots covering their fur. These spots serve as camouflage and help them blend in with their surroundings. Leopard cats have round heads with rounded ears. The colors of the base of their fur varies by the area in which they live. They can vary from a yellowish color to a brownish gray. Their toes are partially webbed on each paw, which helps them swim.

## HABITAT

Leopard cats live in woodland, scrubland, and forest habitats. They don't live in areas with a large amount of snowfall. They are found throughout most of southern Asia. They have the largest range of any wild cat in Asia.

## BEHAVIOR

Leopard cats are usually alone unless it is mating season or mothers are raising their young. During the day they typically spend their time resting in trees. Even though leopard cats are considered nocturnal, they are occasionally active during the day. They are normally very quiet cats, but, on occasion, leopard cats purr or cry like a house cat. They usually hide from humans.

## RAISING YOUNG

Leopard cats have between one and four kittens at a time. The kittens' eyes are closed at birth, and they open them after ten days. Kittens are cared for in a den within a hollow or hollowed-out tree, burrow, or rock crevice. When they become independent, they leave their mothers. By the time they are 18 months old, they are capable of having their own babies.

## PARTICULAR SKILLS

Leopard cats are great climbers and spend a lot of time in trees. They also have excellent hearing and vision. As capable swimmers, they use their partially webbed feet to swim.

## HUNTING HABITS

Leopard cats hunt on the ground and in trees. Their main source of food is mice or rats. They also eat other small mammals, birds, amphibians, lizards, and insects. Leopard cats are ambush hunters that surprise their prey.

## POPULATION

The population of leopard cats is considered stable. They cover a huge range across many countries. Populations are shrinking among certain subspecies in small areas. Some threats to these cats are humans and habitat loss. In some countries they are hunted for their beautiful fur. Farmers sometimes kill the cats because of the fear that they will eat their poultry.

# Marbled Cat

*Pardofelis marmorata*

SOUTH ASIA

## FAST FACTS

**SIZE:** 18 to 24 inches long; 4.4 to 11 pounds

**LIFE SPAN:** Up to 12 years (in captivity)

**FOOD:** Mice, rats, bats, birds, tree squirrels, small primates, lizards, frogs, and insects

**SOUNDS:** Meows that sound like a bird call

## APPEARANCE

Marbled cats are about the size of a domestic cat, but their fur pattern gives them the appearance of clouded leopards. They have beautiful spots on their fur coats. They also have some long dark markings on the crown of their head and down their backs. The base color of their coats can vary from a grayish brown to a yellowish brown to a reddish brown. Their blotches are lighter in the centers and have darker edges. They also have small dark spots and markings on their legs. They have long, thick tails that help them climb by providing extra balance as they travel through trees. Their fur coats are thick and fluffy. Marbled cats have large canine teeth, large padded paws, and small heads.

## HABITAT

Marbled cats can be found in Nepal, northern India, Southeast Asia, Borneo, and Sumatra.

Marbled cats are primarily found in moist tropical forest environments. They find a lot of prey in the forest canopies.

## BEHAVIOR

Very little is known about the behavior of these rare cats. They are one of the least-studied cats in the world. Camera traps have offered some information. However, marbled cats are rarely caught on camera, which may mean that few of these cats are left in the wild.

## PARTICULAR SKILLS

Marbled cats are excellent climbers and spend a lot of time in trees. They can climb headfirst down a tree trunk. They are also able to jump well, which helps them get from branch to branch. They also spend time on land. They have keen low-light vision and are able to see well in the dark.

## HUNTING HABITS

Marbled cats hunt on land and up in treetops. They eat mice, rats, bats, birds, tree squirrels, and small primates. They also eat lizards, frogs, and insects.

## RAISING YOUNG

There is very little information about how their young are raised in the wild. Researchers observed two litters born in captivity. Each litter had two kittens. The kittens ate solid foods at about 2 months old, which was also when they were able to start climbing.

## POPULATION

The population of marbled cats is declining and considered to be highly threatened. Since this cat is dependent on its forest habitat, habitat loss is a major threat. Deforestation from human population growth and logging are shrinking their habitat.

# Margay

*Leopardus wiedii*

CENTRAL AND SOUTH AMERICA

## FAST FACTS

**SIZE:** 18 to 27 inches long; 5 to 11 pounds

**LIFE SPAN:** Over 20 years (in captivity)

**FOOD:** Birds, tamarins, rats, mice, rabbits, amphibians, and reptiles

**SOUNDS:** A variety of sounds, including ones that mimic their prey

# APPEARANCE

Margays are slightly larger than a typical house cat and have spotted fur coats. Their tawny fur is covered with dark spots and rosettes. The rosettes have dark edges with light-colored centers. Margays have large eyes and long tails. Since they look like ocelots and spend so much time in trees, they are sometimes referred to as tree ocelots.

# HABITAT

Margays are mostly found in forest habitats. They prefer to live in places with a lot of tree cover. They can be found in 19 different countries in both North and South America.

# BEHAVIOR

Margays are solitary cats. They are mostly active during the night. Even though margays spend a lot of their time in trees, they also hunt and travel on land. When it comes to hunting, they tend not to stalk prey. Margays prefer to wait until they come near and surprise them with an ambush.

# RAISING YOUNG

Margay mothers usually give birth to just one or two kittens at a time. Mothers often choose hollowed-out logs as dens for raising their kittens. Kittens can open their eyes at around 2 weeks old. They are able to start eating solid food by the time they are around 8 weeks old.

# PARTICULAR SKILLS

Margays are excellent climbers. They have many adaptations that help them live in trees. They can rotate their ankles 180 degrees. The rotating ankles allow them to walk down trees facing forward. They can grasp trees well with their paws. They can even climb upside down on a branch! Their large soft feet and toes allow them to hang upside down from one paw. Margays can jump up to 12 feet, which helps them leap from branch to branch. Their large eyes help them see at night.

## HUNTING HABITS

Since they are so agile in trees, margays do a lot of their hunting in trees. They eat birds, tamarins, rats, mice, rabbits, amphibians, and reptiles. A camera captured a margay mimicking the sound of a crying tamarin baby to lure a tamarin as prey. Even though the monkey escaped, it showed that the margay was smart enough to come up with a way to trick the tamarin.

## POPULATION

The population of margays is decreasing. The threats to these cats are habitat loss and humans. Margays are hunted for their beautiful fur. Since they only have one or two kittens each year, it is difficult to rebuild the population.

# Ocelot

*Leopardus pardalis*

NORTH AND
SOUTH AMERICA

## FAST FACTS

**SIZE:** 28 to 35 inches long; 24 to 35 pounds

**LIFE SPAN:** Over 20 years (in captivity)

**FOOD:** Frogs, iguanas, rabbits, fish, crabs, rodents, monkeys, and birds

**SOUNDS:** Purrs, hisses, snarls, growls, chuckles, mutters, and yowls

## APPEARANCE

Ocelots are about twice the size of a house cat. They have beautiful sleek fur coats and long tails. Their gold fur has dark spots and blotches.

## HABITAT

Ocelots cover a large range from North America to South America. They can be found in a variety of different habitats. They thrive in scrublands all the way to tropical rain forests. But wherever they choose to live, it's always in an area with a lot of plants to provide cover for stealthy hunting.

## BEHAVIOR

Ocelots are nocturnal cats that hunt at night. They have excellent night vision that helps them see well in the dark. During the day they rest in trees or hide in vegetation on the ground. They spend most of their adult lives alone.

## RAISING YOUNG

Females have between one and four kittens in each litter. The babies already have spots and markings when they are born. They are born with blue eyes, but they turn brown in just a few months. By 8 weeks old, they are able to start eating meat. Ocelot kittens learn how to hunt from their mothers.

## PARTICULAR SKILLS

Ocelots have sharp fangs that deliver a fatal bite to their prey. They do not have teeth designed for chewing food. Instead, their teeth work well for tearing meat into pieces small enough that they can swallow it. Like many cats, they have great vision and hearing. These cats are also good swimmers.

## HUNTING HABITS

Ocelots do most of their hunting on land, but they can also hunt in trees. Some of the animals they eat are frogs, iguanas, rabbits, fish, crabs, rodents, monkeys, and birds.

## POPULATION

Overall, the population of ocelots is not considered endangered. But there are some areas in which the population is at risk. Habitat loss is a big threat for ocelots because without enough plants and trees to provide cover, they can't survive and leave an area. Ocelots used to be hunted for their beautiful fur, but are now protected in most of their native countries.

# Oncilla

*Leopardus tigrinus*

CENTRAL AND
SOUTH AMERICA

## FAST FACTS

**SIZE:** 15 to 23 inches long; 3.3 to 6.6 pounds

**FOOD:** Small mammals, lizards, and birds

**LIFE SPAN:** 10 to 14 years; over 20 years in captivity

**SOUNDS:** Purrs and gurgles

## APPEARANCE

Oncillas have beautiful fur that is golden brown to gray with dark rosette spots. Their rosettes have a darker outline with light brown in the center. Their tails have dark rings around them. Their eyes range from a honey color to a darker brown. There are also some oncillas that have all dark fur, but they are usually found in dense forests.

They look similar to the margays and ocelots that also live in South America. Oncillas are often called *tigrillo* or "little tiger cat."

## HABITAT

Oncillas mostly live in South America, but there are small populations in parts of Central America. These cats are most often found living in forest habitats but also live in savannas or scrubland habitats.

## BEHAVIOR

While these cats are mostly nocturnal, they will also hunt during the day if their prey is active during daytime hours. They are solitary cats and spend most of their adult lives alone. Oncillas spend most of their time on land but are excellent climbers and can escape a threat by quickly climbing a tree.

## RAISING YOUNG

There is very little known about how oncillas mate and raise young in the wild. From observations in captivity, researchers have been able to learn about how these cats raise their young. Mothers usually only have one kitten at a time, but occasionally can have up to three kittens. At around 3 weeks old, all of their teeth grow in at the same time. By 4 months of age the kittens are independent and ready to take care of themselves.

## HUNTING HABITS

Oncillas usually eat small mammals, lizards, and birds. They remove the feathers from a bird before eating it. To kill their prey, they bite the back of its neck.

## POPULATION

The population of oncillas is listed as vulnerable. They have been heavily hunted in the past for their beautiful spotted fur. Habitat loss is also a big threat to these small wild cats.

# Pallas's Cat

*Otocolobus manul*

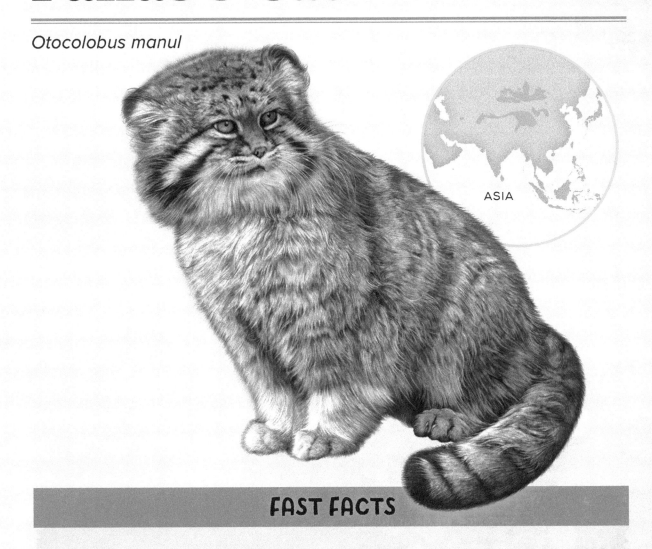

ASIA

## FAST FACTS

**SIZE:** 18 to 26 inches long; 5 to 13 pounds

**LIFE SPAN:** Up to 12 years (in captivity)

**FOOD:** Rodents and pikas

**SOUNDS:** Yelps, purrs, and growls

## APPEARANCE

These cats are actually about the size of a house cat, but their superlong, fluffy fur makes them look a lot larger. They have flat faces and long bushy tails. Pallas's cats have the thickest fur of any cat species. It changes color with the season, which helps them to blend in with their surroundings. In the summer months, their fur is a brownish red tint with stripes, and in the winter, it is a solid gray.

## HISTORY

The Pallas's cat was originally discovered by a German naturalist named Peter Pallas in 1776. He called it *Felis manul*. Today the scientific name for this cat is *Otocolobus manul*. *Otocolobus* is a Greek word that means "ugly eared." Their ears are unusually low on the sides of their heads. This feature probably help them when hiding.

## HABITAT

Pallas's cats live in small caves, rock crevices, or the abandoned dens of other animals. Their habitat is dry, rocky **steppes** and grasslands as high as 15,000 feet. Living at such a high altitude on the mountains means cold temperatures. Luckily, Pallas's cats have extremely thick fur to help them stay warm in the extremely cold temperatures, which can drop to −60°F!

## BEHAVIOR

These cats are solitary besides when they are mating or raising their babies. They are crepuscular, which means they are most active at dusk and dawn when they are out hunting.

## RAISING YOUNG

Pallas's cats can have up to eight kittens per litter. At around 2 months old, the kittens molt, shedding their baby fur. Then they grow their thick adult coats. Once they have adult fur, they leave the den to follow their mother. The mother teaches them how to hunt and take care of themselves before they venture off on their own.

## HUNTING HABITS

Pallas's cats are not speedy runners. They are ambush hunters and surprise their prey with a sneaky attack. They stalk their prey and stay hidden in the grass and rocks until they are ready to pounce. Pallas's cats hunt rodents and birds. One of their favorite foods is pika.

## POPULATION

These rare cats are considered near threatened on the endangered species list. One of the biggest threats to these cats is losing their food source. Locals poison the rodents and pikas that Pallas's cats eat, and this reduces their food supply. Sometimes the cats accidentally eat the poisoned animals, which then kills them.

# Pampas Cat

*Leopardus colocolo*

SOUTH AMERICA

## FAST FACTS

**SIZE:** 16.5 to 31 inches long; 6.6 to 9 pounds

**LIFE SPAN:** 9 to 18 years

**FOOD:** Guinea pigs and other rodents

**SOUNDS:** Hisses, spits, growls, meows, gurgles, and purrs

## APPEARANCE

Pampas cats have a variety of different looks, and their appearance is based on where they live. They are about the size of a house cat, but look larger because of their long, puffy hair and wide face. They come in a variety of colors and patterns. Some have stripes or markings on their fur, while others are a solid color. Their fur can be a pale yellow, gray, light brown, or reddish. They have pink noses and a short, fluffy tail.

## HABITAT

Pampas cats live in a lot of different habitats in South America. They can be found in grasslands, **cloud forests**, open woodlands, swampy areas, and savannas.

## BEHAVIOR

Pampas cats live and hunt on land. They are also great climbers. When intimidated, the hair down the center of their backs stands up, which makes them look larger.

There is very little known about the behavior of these cats in the wild.

## RAISING YOUNG

Based on what researchers have observed in pampas cats in captivity, these wild cats have between one and three kittens per litter. Like other cats, the mothers provide milk to their babies until they are old enough to hunt and eat meat.

## HUNTING HABITS

Pampas cats hunt small animals like guinea pigs and other rodents. They have been known to hunt ground-dwelling birds and have been seen eating penguin eggs.

## POPULATION

The pampas cat population is at risk and is considered near threatened on the endangered animal list. Habitat loss is a large threat because much of the grassland that they used to inhabit has been turned into cropland and grazing for livestock.

# Rusty-spotted Cat

*Prionailurus rubiginosus*

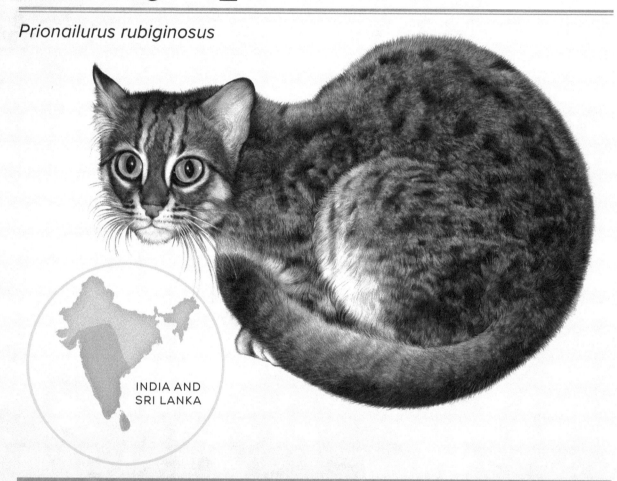

INDIA AND
SRI LANKA

## FAST FACTS

**SIZE:** 13 to 19 inches long; 2 to 3.5 pounds

**LIFE SPAN:** Up to 12 years (in captivity)

**FOOD:** Birds, lizards, frogs, and insects

**SOUNDS:** Unknown

## APPEARANCE

Rusty-spotted cats are one of the world's smallest wild cats. They're only about half the size of a house cat! They have grayish brown fur with rust-colored markings and dark stripes. Their creamy white bellies are also marked with dark spots and stripes. Rusty-spotted cats have large eyes that help them see in the dark.

## HABITAT

Rusty-spotted cats live in areas with thick vegetation or rocky areas. They are found in different types of forests, grasslands, and rocky locations. They live in India and Sri Lanka.

## BEHAVIOR

There is very little information about rusty-spotted cats' behavior in the wild. They are thought to be nocturnal as most sightings have been at night. They can quickly climb a tree or hide in between rocks to hide. During the day they rest in well-hidden areas such as hollow or hollowed-out logs or thick vegetation.

## RAISING YOUNG

Female rusty-spotted cats have one to three kittens per litter. They have their kittens in a secluded spot like a den or cave. The newborn kittens are so small that they weigh less than a chicken egg when born! When the kittens are born, they have rows of black spots. Their fur changes to a reddish-brown rust coloring as they grow into adults.

## HUNTING HABITS

Rusty-spotted cats are most active at night. They eat mostly rodents, but they will also hunt birds, lizards, frogs, and insects. They are agile and quick hunters. They use their speed to quickly snag their prey.

## POPULATION

The population of these cats is vulnerable and shrinking. The biggest threat to these cats is habitat loss.

# Sand Cat

*Felis margarita*

ASIA AND AFRICA

## FAST FACTS

**SIZE:** 15 to 20 inches long; 3 to 7.5 pounds

**LIFE SPAN:** Up to 13 years (in captivity)

**FOOD:** Rodents, hares, snakes, birds, spiders, and reptiles

**SOUNDS:** Meows, growls, hisses, spits, screams, and purrs

## APPEARANCE

Sand cats' fur coats are designed to help them blend in with their sandy environment. They have sandy- to gray-colored fur with faint stripes. Reddish streaks cross their faces near their eyes. Their tails have dark rings and black tips. Sand cats have large ears that sit low on the sides of their heads. Having their ears low helps them hide when they are crouching in sand.

## HABITAT

Sand cats are built to live in the desert. They live in dry deserts with little vegetation in Africa and Asia. The desert can get very hot during the day and very cold at night. Their thick fur helps protect them from these extreme weather conditions.

## BEHAVIOR

Sand cats are mostly nocturnal and crepuscular. They rest in burrows to avoid the heat of the daytime. They are solitary cats unless females are raising their young. They have been known to use the same burrows as other sand cats, although never at the same time.

## RAISING YOUNG

Sand cats can have from one to eight kittens in each litter. The kittens are tiny at birth, weighing just over an ounce! Kittens stay with their mothers while they learn how to survive on their own. They become independent between 6 and 8 months old.

## PARTICULAR SKILLS

Sand cats are great diggers. Their oversized ears help them hear the tiniest sounds made by prey. They listen for prey burrowing underground, then quickly dig them out. They also dig burrows to hide from the heat and cold. Their paws are covered in long, thick fur and have special pads to protect them from the harsh elements of the desert.

## HUNTING HABITS

Since food can be hard to find in the desert, these cats are opportunistic hunters and will hunt what is available. They mostly eat rodents, but they will also eat hares, snakes, birds, spiders, and reptiles. They even eat venomous snakes! Sand cats get the water they need from prey so they can go weeks at a time without drinking water. If they catch more meat than they can eat, sand cats bury the rest under the sand to save for a later meal.

## POPULATION

The population of sand cats isn't currently considered at risk for extinction and is listed as of least concern on the IUCN Red List. Their biggest threat is habitat loss and loss of prey. If the little vegetation that naturally occurs in the desert goes away, then the small animals that the sand cats eat will decrease.

# Serval

*Leptailurus serval*

AFRICA

## FAST FACTS

**SIZE:** 23 to 36 inches long; 15 to 40 pounds

**LIFE SPAN:** Up to 19 years (in captivity)

**FOOD:** Rodents, birds, reptiles, crabs, frogs, fish, and large insects

**SOUNDS:** Growls, meows, shrill cries, hisses, and purrs

## APPEARANCE

Servals are medium-sized cats with long, slender bodies. For their body size, servals have the longest legs and largest ears of any cat. Their pale yellow coats have black spots and stripes. Their tails are short and often include dark rings with solid black tips.

## HABITAT

Servals are found in many countries in Africa. They live in savannas that have plenty of water. They can also be found in dry reed beds near streams, bamboo thickets, and environments with bushes and tall grasses. Their long legs and necks help them see above the tall grass of the savanna.

## BEHAVIOR

Servals are solitary cats that spend most of their adult lives by themselves. They are active during the day but avoid the hottest part of the day. They mostly hunt in the mornings and evenings. Occasionally they hunt at night.

## RAISING YOUNG

Servals can have between one and five kittens in each litter. Females keep their kittens well-hidden in tall grass or dens. The mother will leave the kittens in the dens during the day while she hunts, then return to care for them. By the time they are 6 months old, their sharp canine teeth come in.

## HUNTING HABITS

Servals are great hunters and succeed in about half of their hunting attempts. They have a much higher hunting success rate than most cats. They use a variety of hunting methods to catch prey. Servals use their large ears to listen for prey as they wait in the tall grass. Then they do a huge leap to pounce on top of the animal, delivering a strong bite to the neck. They also sometimes reach their long front legs into a rodent hole to snag a meal. Another hunting strategy is dipping their sharp curved claws into the water to spear a fish or frog. Their long legs let them leap more than 9 feet into the air to snatch flying birds! Servals' legs are also built for speed. They can sprint up to 50 miles per hour. Servals eat a variety of animals including rodents, birds, reptiles, crabs, frogs, fish, and large insects.

## POPULATION

The population of servals is not considered endangered. This means that there are enough servals in the wild that experts don't believe they are at risk for extinction. Like other wild cats, habitat loss is one of the biggest threats to servals. Their predators include leopards, wild dogs, hyenas, and humans.

# Wildcat

*Felis silvestris*

EUROPE, ASIA,
AND AFRICA

## FAST FACTS

**SIZE:** 16 to 36 inches long; 6 to 18 pounds

**FOOD:** Mice, rats, birds, ducks, and hares

**LIFE SPAN:** Up to 15 years

**SOUNDS:** Hisses, yowls, purrs, and squeaks

-THE BIG BOOK OF WILD CATS-

## APPEARANCE

Wildcats are larger than a typical house cat. In appearance they look a lot like a tabby cat with gray or light brown fur with dark stripes. They have pointed ears and long whiskers sticking out of their cheeks. Their bushy tails have dark stripes and black tips.

## HABITAT

Wildcats are found in many countries in Europe, Asia, and Africa. Wildcats in Europe usually live in and around forests. Wildcats in Africa are usually found in areas around water and mountains but can be found in other habitats except for tropical rain forests. In Asia, wildcats can be found in scrubland deserts and a variety of other habitats.

## BEHAVIOR

Wildcats are mostly solitary unless they are breeding or raising kittens. Even though these cats will rest in dens, they don't dig their own. They find the abandoned dens of other animals or hollow or hollowed-out logs for shelter.

## RAISING YOUNG

Wildcat mothers usually have between one and seven kittens in each litter. The babies are born blind and helpless and depend completely on their mothers. At around 2 months old, they start hunting with their mother. At around 5 months old, kittens venture off on their own.

## HUNTING HABITS

Wildcats mostly eat rodents like mice and rats. But they will also eat birds, ducks, hares, and other small animals. Because they are so helpful in controlling rodent populations, this is probably the species that led people to consider keeping cats as pets. When wildcats hunt ducks and other prey in the water, they will climb out on a branch that hangs over the water and reach out with a claw to snatch their prey.

## PARTICULAR SKILLS

Wildcats have an excellent sense of hearing. They can hear the tiny sounds of rodents, which can help them find their prey before they see it. Wildcats' whiskers are also important to their senses. They use their whiskers to "feel" the size of openings to make sure they fit before attempting to enter small spaces.

## POPULATION

The population of wildcats is currently stable and considered to be of least concern on the IUCN Red List. Wildcats in Africa and Asia have steady populations. The European wildcat population seems to be declining due to habitat loss, being hit by cars, and catching diseases from domestic cats. Predators to young wildcats are foxes, wolves, owls, and hawks. Wildcats are feisty and will fight hard to defend themselves against predators.

Ocelot

# KITTY CATS

There are many different species of wild cats, but all domestic cats belong to the same species: Felis catus. Within that species, there are different types of domestic cats that scientists classify into breeds. In the United States there are around 90 million domestic cats, showing how beloved these pets are. Most likely today's domestic cats are descendants of the Middle Eastern wildcat.

Based on evidence found in Egypt, people may have started keeping cats as pets as long as 4,000 years ago. Ancient Egyptians worshipped a cat goddess and mummified cat remains. In addition, a lot of art based on cats has been found from ancient Egyptian times. Cat skeletons found on the island of Cyprus make scientists believe that humans may have started keeping cats as pets more than 8,000 years ago. In Cyprus, a cat and human skeleton were found buried together. This discovery suggested to scientists that humans and cats must have had a close relationship during that time period.

MUMMIFIED CAT

People probably became interested in cats due to their ability to hunt rodents. Having cats around probably helped them keep mice and rats out of their homes and crops. When people started having large farms and began harvesting and storing large amounts of grain and food, those storages attracted rodents. The larger number of rodents probably drew small wild cats into the more populated areas.

DOMESTIC CAT CATCHING A RODENT

People probably noticed that cats were excellent rodent hunters and could protect the food from rodent damage.

# ENDANGERED CATS

Many species of cats are considered endangered, which means that they are at risk of becoming extinct. When an animal becomes extinct, that means there are no longer any of those animals alive in the world. Tigers, snow leopards, and Iberian lynx are just a few of the cats on the endangered species list. The IUCN keeps a list of all the animals and their risk for extinction.

# How You Can Help

One of the biggest threats to endangered animals is habitat loss. When there is reduced space for their range and less prey, they cannot survive. To help animals, it is important that we take care of Earth and keep their environments safe. Make sure you clean up your trash and do not waste water. Always reduce, reuse, and recycle items in order to help the environment. Plant bushes and trees to provide shelter and cover for animals. Respecting and taking care of nature is a great way to help keep their habitat safe.

Another way that you can help is to learn about each of the endangered animals in your area. This way you can find out what must be done to protect them. You can also teach your friends and family about the facts you learn. Understanding these amazing creatures helps us realize why they are so important to our world. You can go to wildlife parks or refuges and get more information from park rangers about how you can help.

# MAPS

CANADA LYNX

BOBCAT

COUGAR

JAGUAR

JAGUARUNDI

OCELOT

ONCILLA

MARGAY

# SOUTH AMERICA

JAGUARUNDI

JAGUAR

ONCILLA

PAMPAS CAT

COUGAR

MARGAY

OCELOT

KODKOD

GEOFFROY'S CAT

ANDEAN
MOUNTAIN CAT

MAPS

# EUROPE

EURASIAN
LYNX

WILDCAT

IBERIAN
LYNX

MAPS

# ASIA

SNOW LEOPARD

CLOUDED LEOPARD

ASIAN
GOLDEN C AT

EURASIAN
LYNX

CHEETAH

TIGER

JUNGLE CAT

CHINESE
MOUNTAIN CAT

SAND CAT

WILDCAT

FISHING CAT

CARACAL

SUNDA
CLOUDED LEOPARD

PALLAS'S CAT

LION

LEOPARD CAT

FLAT-HEADED CAT

MARBLED CAT

RUSTY-SPOTTED
CAT

LEOPARD

BORNEO
BAY CAT

# AFRICA

WILDCAT

SERVAL

SAND CAT

LION

CHEETAH

LEOPARD

CARACAL

BLACK-FOOTED CAT

JUNGLE CAT

AFRICAN
GOLDEN CAT

MAPS

# Glossary

abandoned: given up or deserted

adaptation: a change that causes a species to be better suited to its environment

carnivore: an animal that eats meat

cloud forest: a damp evergreen forest that is frequently covered by low-lying clouds

crepuscular: active at the time of day just before the sun goes down or just after the sun rises

diurnal: active during the day

domestic: an animal tamed and kept by humans

elusive: difficult to find

endangered: at risk of extinction

grassland: a large open area of country covered with grass

habitat: the natural home or environment of an animal or plant

nocturnal: active at night

pika: a small mammal with short ears and hind legs; related to rabbits

predator: an animal that kills and eats other animals

rain forest: a tropical forest, usually with tall, densely growing, broad-leaved trees in an area with a lot of rainfall

savanna: a grassy plain in tropical and subtropical regions that has few trees

**scrubland:** land consisting of stunted trees and shrub vegetation

**solitary:** living alone without companions

**species:** the basic category of biological classification; composed of related individuals that resemble one another and are able to reproduce with each other

**steppe:** a large area of flat, unforested grassland

**prey:** an animal that is killed by another for food

**vegetation:** the type of plants found in a particular area or habitat

**vole:** a rodent with a stout body and short ears; related to muskrats

# About the Author

Rachael Smith is the founder and curriculum designer of the website Literacy with the Littles (LiteracyWithTheLittles.com). Through her blog, she shares crafts and educational activities for parents and teachers that are designed to help little ones develop a love of learning. In 2010, she earned her bachelor's degree in early childhood education and began her teaching career. Rachael is a former first-grade teacher turned stay-at-home mom. She is a wife and the mother of four little ones. She enjoys crafting, traveling, sports, spending time outdoors, and making memories with her family.

CPSIA information can be obtained
at www.ICGtesting.com
Printed in the USA
LVHW070156280220
648471LV00002B/3

9 781646 110605